What Do You See?

By Jacqui Briggs

Illustrated by Pamela Anzalotti

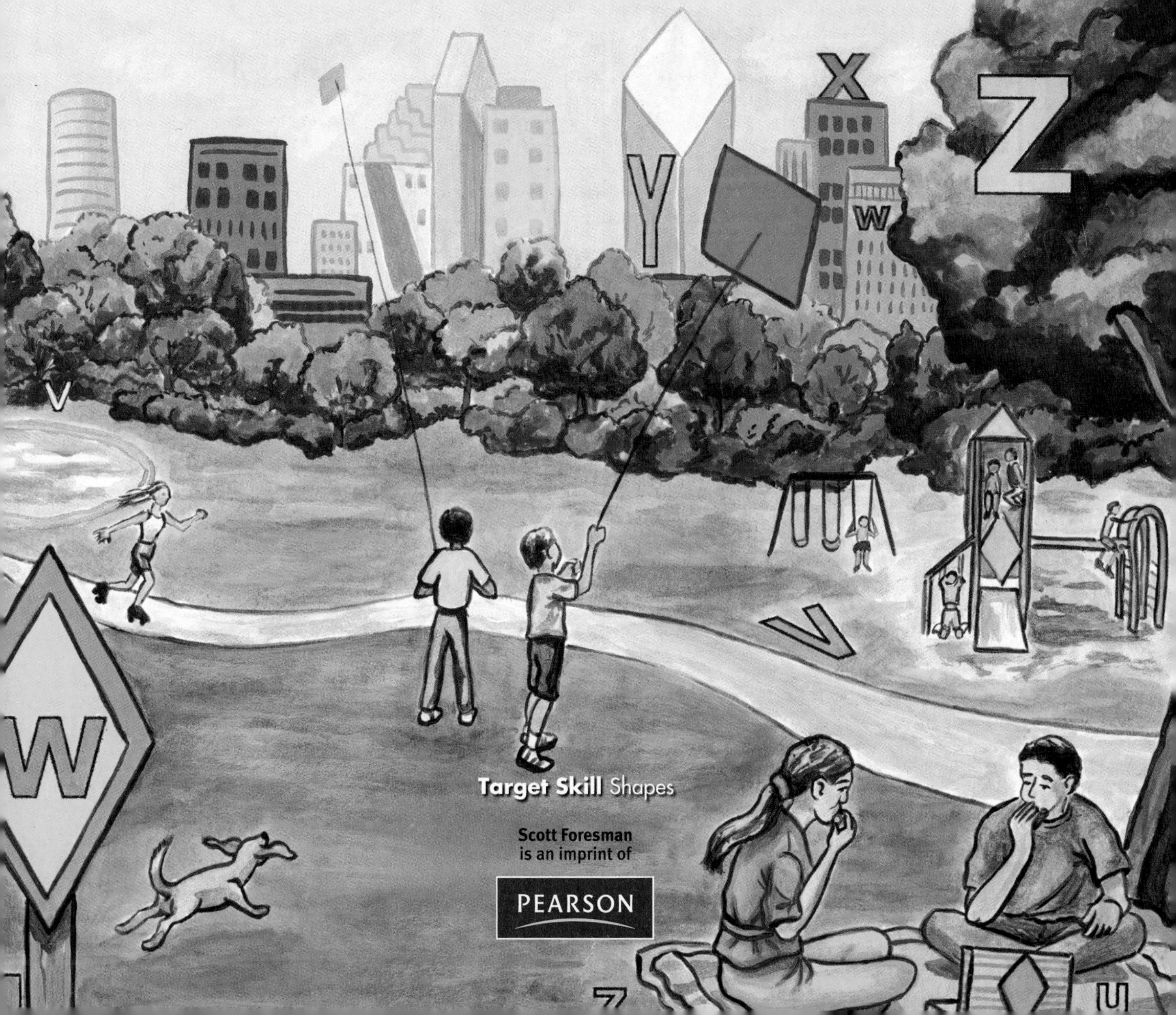

Target Skill Shapes

Scott Foresman
is an imprint of

PEARSON

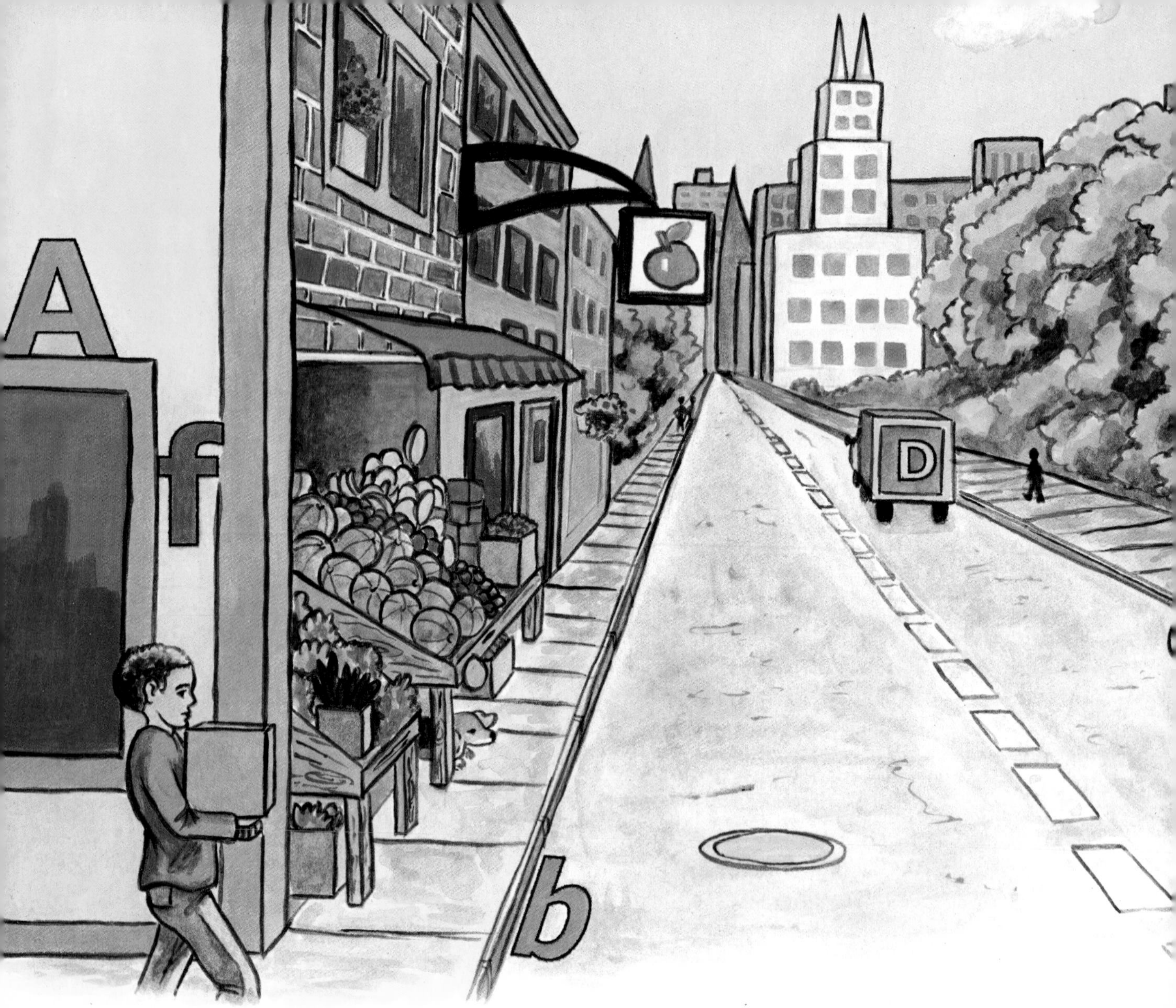

square

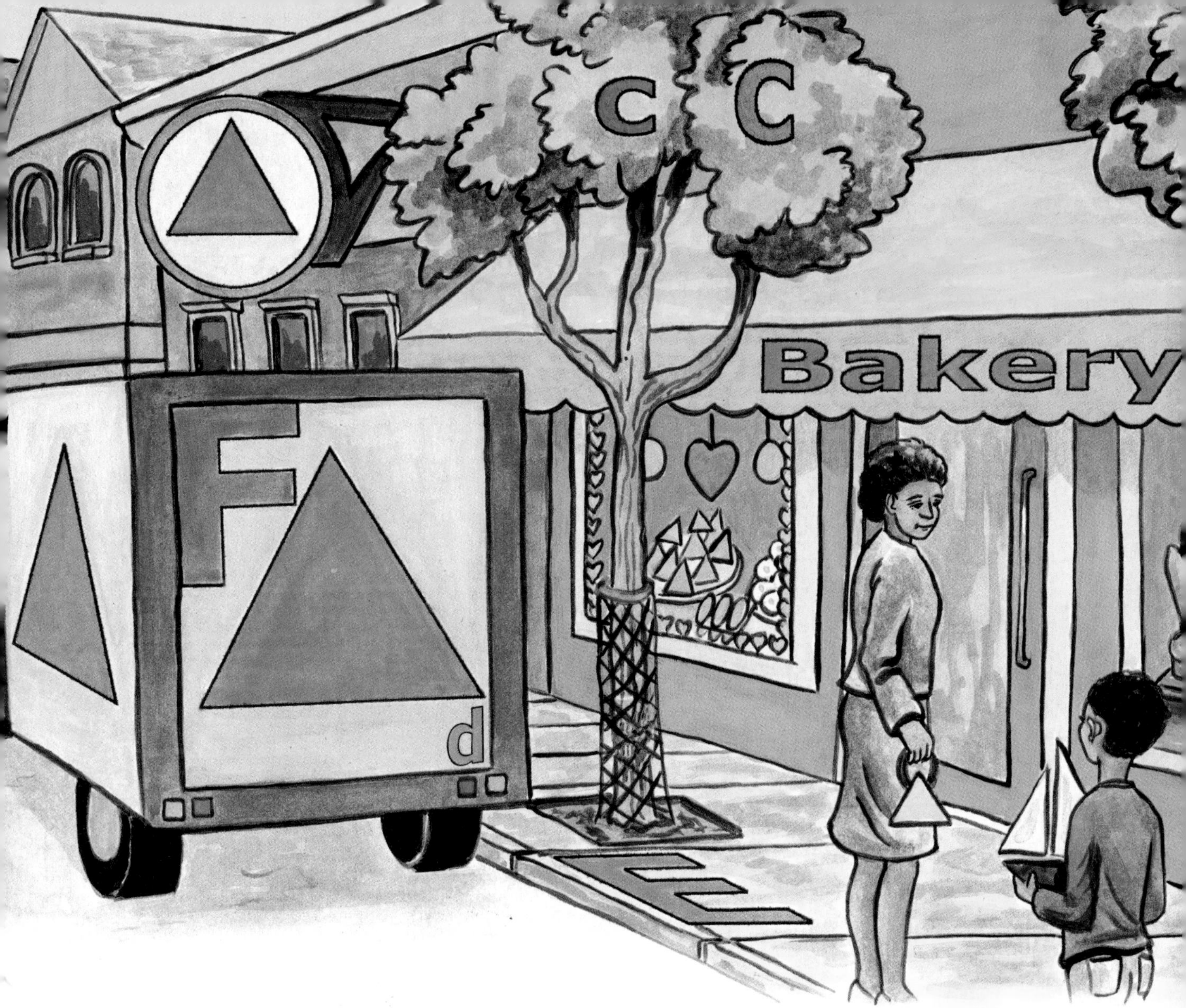

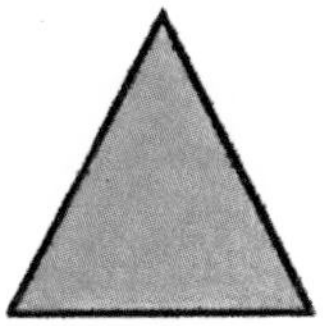

triangle

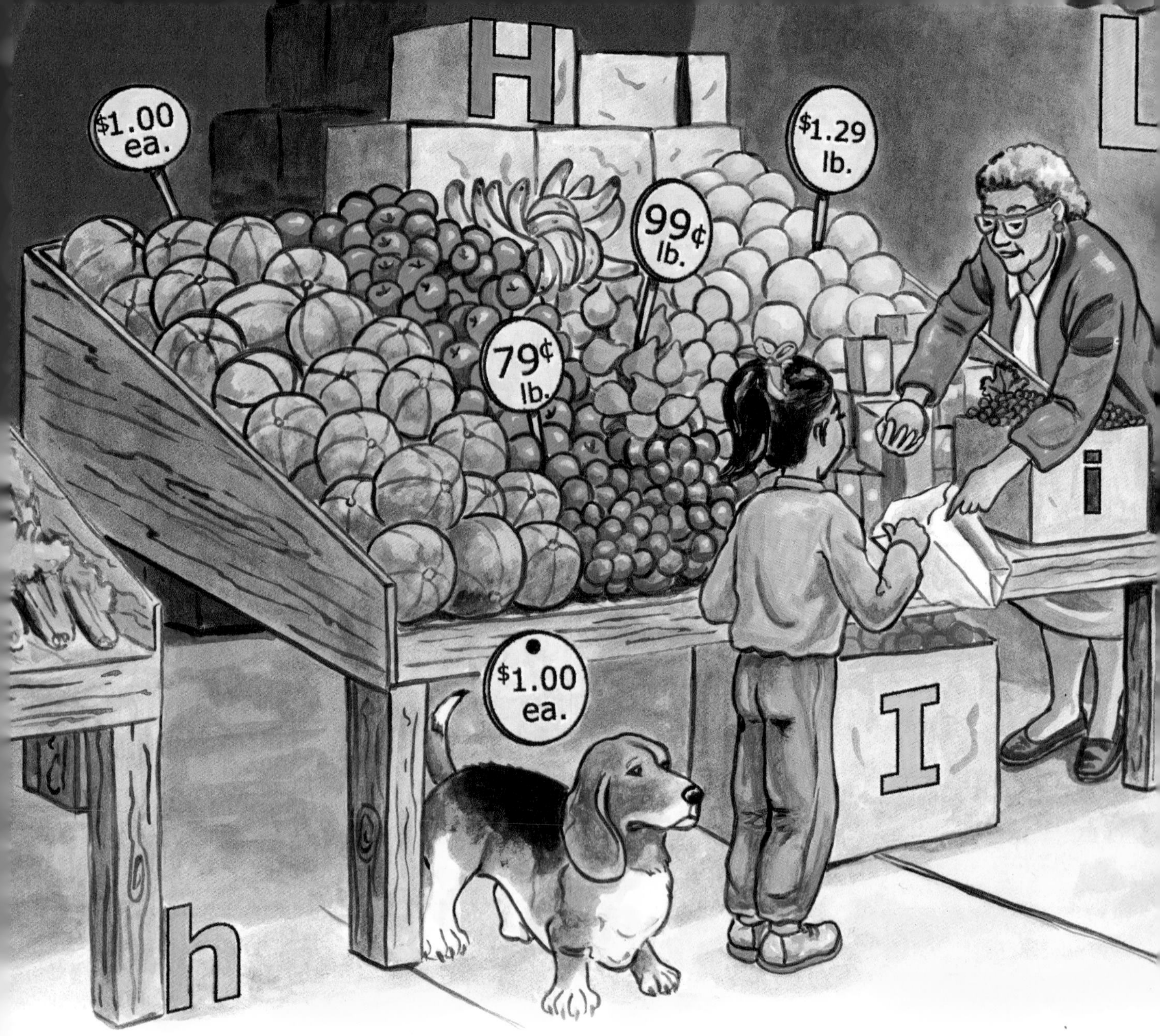

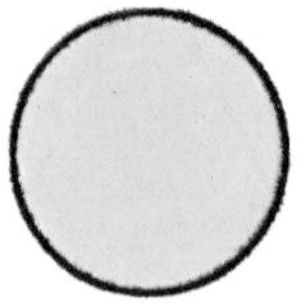

circle

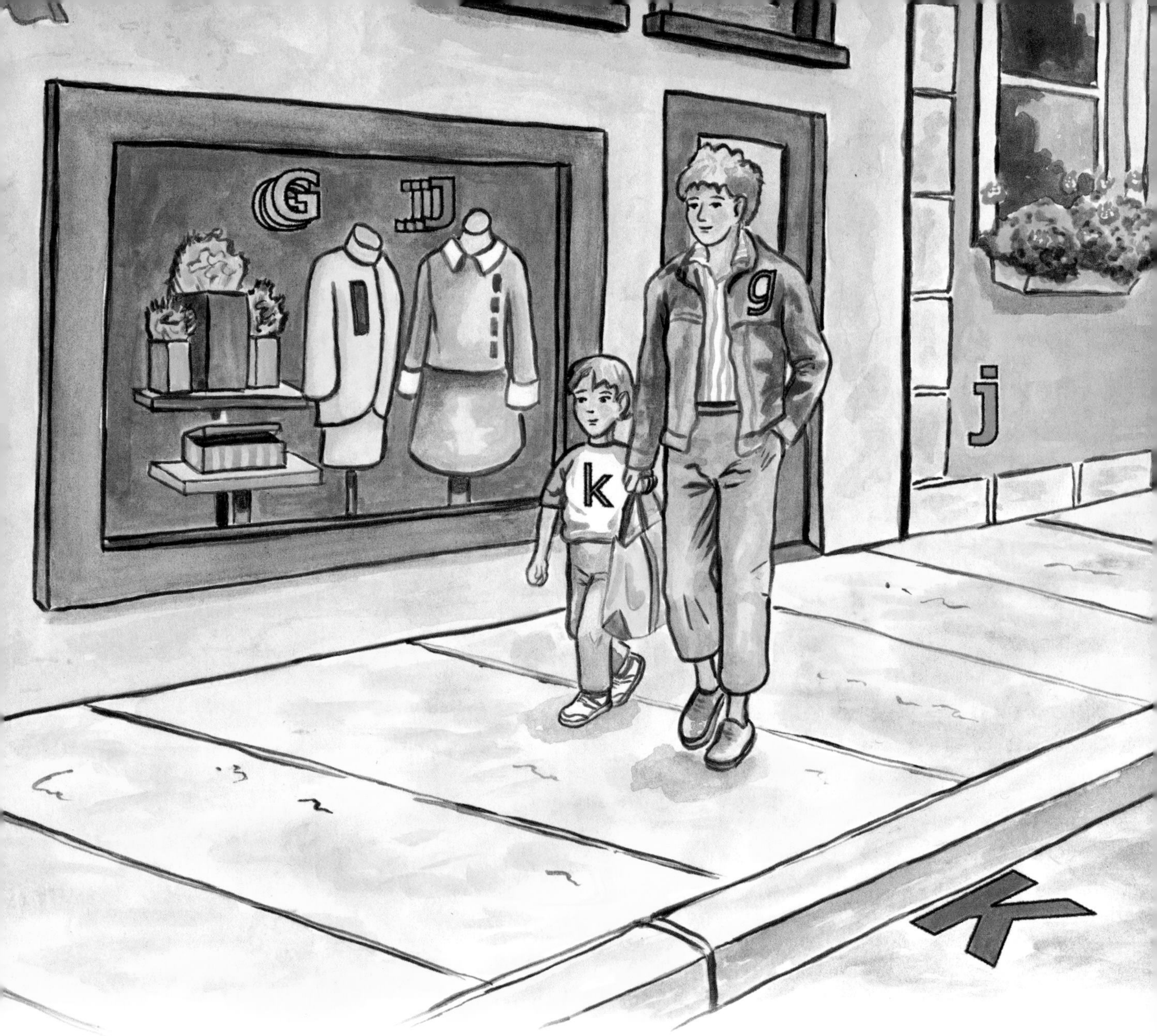

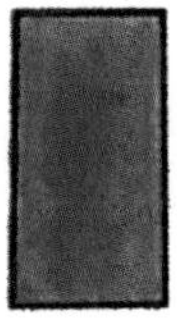

rectangle

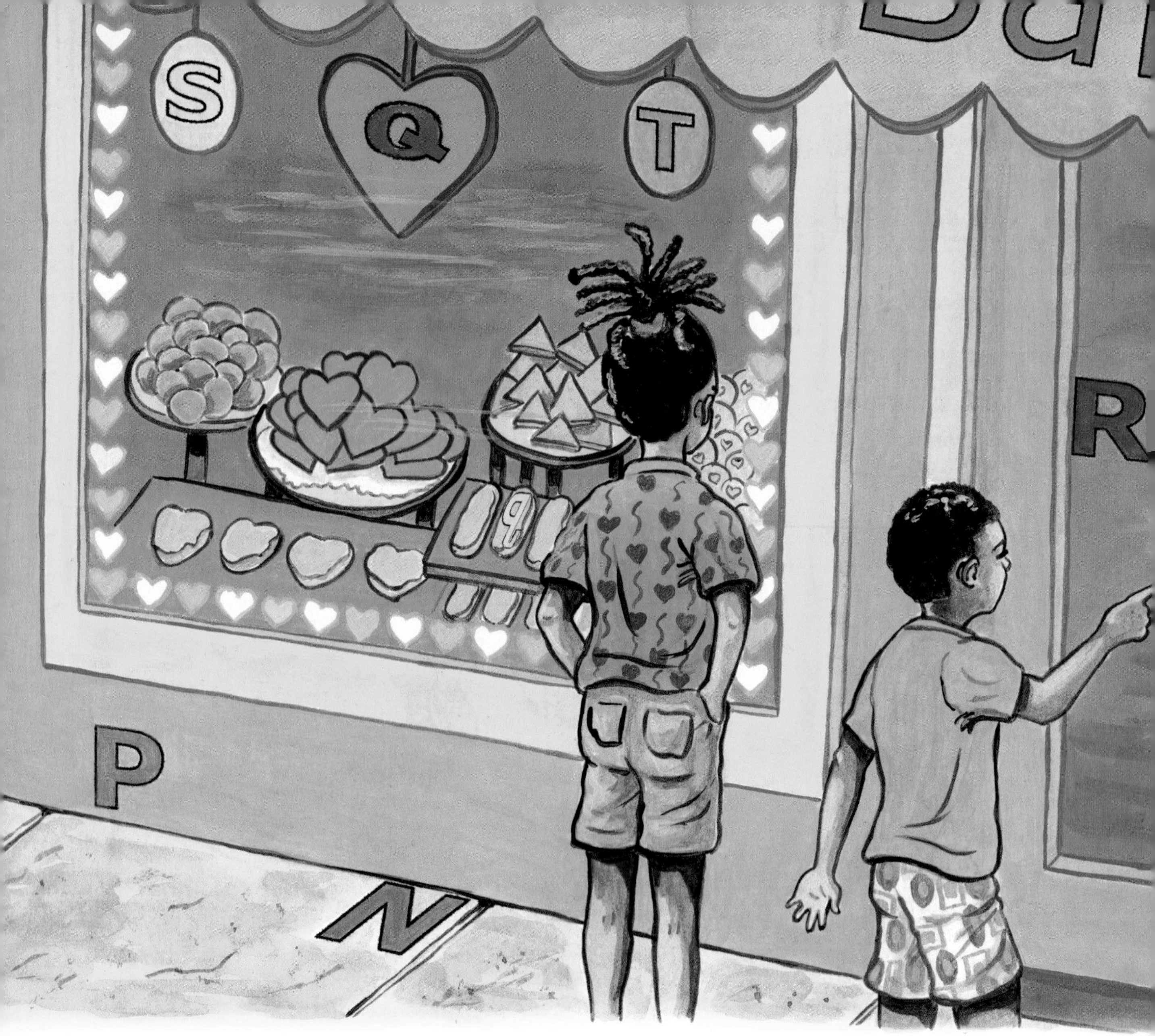

heart

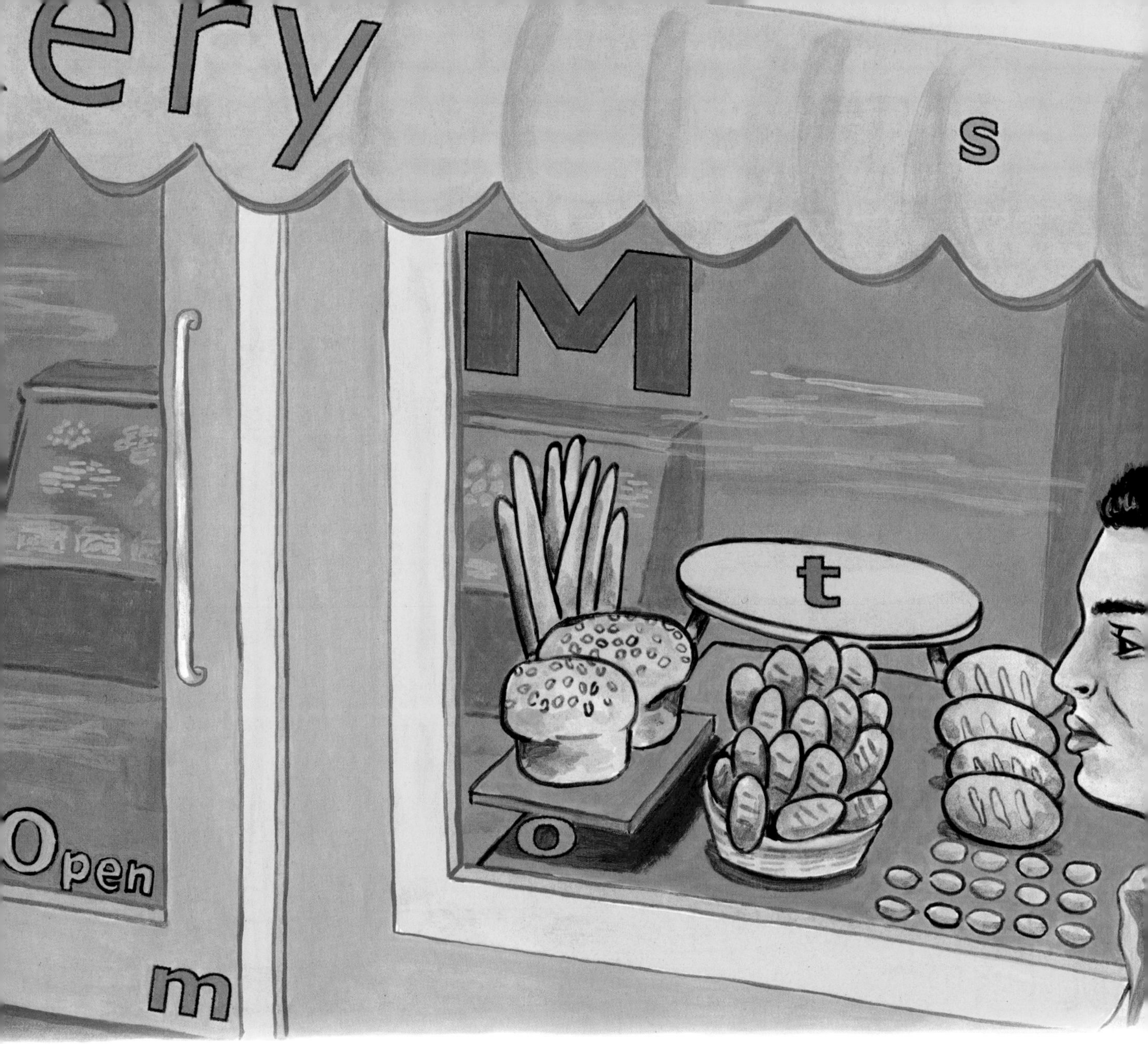

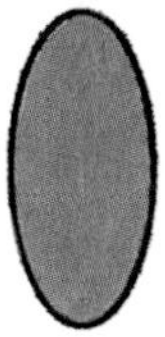

oval

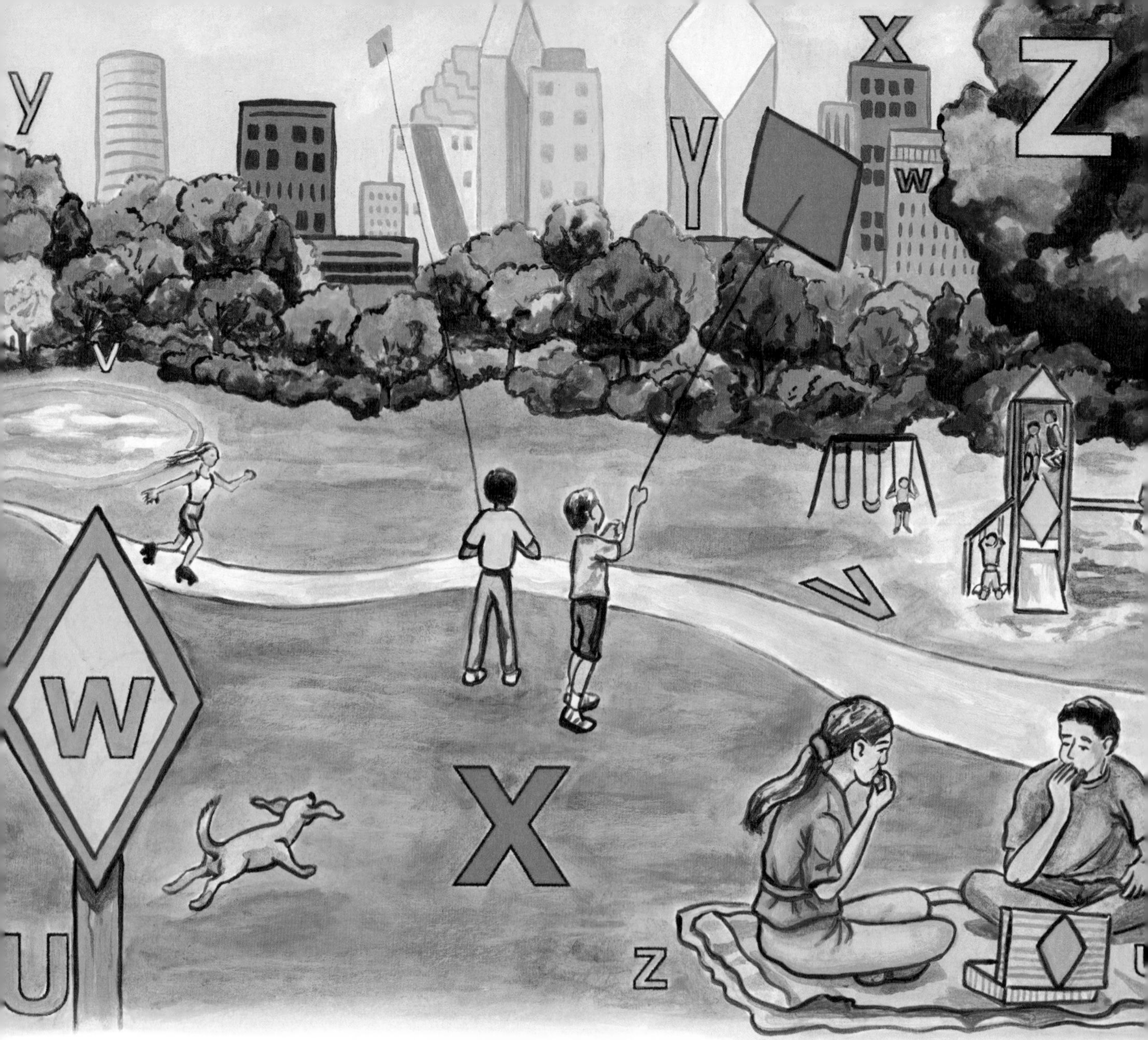
Y
X
Y
Z
W
V
V
W
X
U
Z

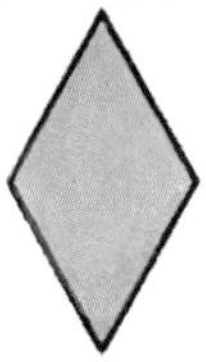

diamond